Natural Histories

EMILY HASLER was born in Felixstowe, Suffolk and studied at the University of Warwick for a BA in English Literature and Creative Writing and an MA in Romanticism. She now lives in London. In 2009 she won second prize in the Edwin Morgan International Poetry Competition. Her poems have appeared in various publications, including *The Rialto*, *Poetry Salzburg*, *Warwick Review* and *Horizon Review*, and have been anthologised in *Dove Release*, *Birdbook*, *Clinic 2* and *Herbarium*. Her poems will also appear in *The Salt Book of Younger Poets* and *The Best British Poetry 2011*. She is a regular poetry reviewer for *Warwick Review*.

I0087678

Natural Histories

by

EMILY HASLER

SALT

LONDON

PUBLISHED BY SALT PUBLISHING
Acre House, 11–15 William Road, London NW1 3ER, United Kingdom

© Emily Hasler, 2011

The right of Emily Hasler to be identified as the
author of this work has been asserted by her in accordance
with Section 77 of the Copyright, Designs and Patents Act 1988.

Salt Publishing 2011

Printed and bound in the United Kingdom by Lightning Source UK Ltd

Typeset in Swift 9.5 / 13

ISBN 978 1 84471 867 2 pamphlet

1 3 5 7 9 8 6 4 2

for Jen and Chris

Contents

Acknowledgements

I would like to thank the following magazines, websites and publications where some of these poems first appeared: *Birdbook* (Sidekick Books), *Clinic 2*, *Horizon Review*, *Days of Roses*, the Wordsworth Trust newsletter, and *Dove Release* (Worple Press 2010).

I would also like to thank the following people for so kindly giving their invaluable support and advice: Polly Atkin, Paul Batchelor, James Brookes, Andrew Forster, David Morley, Eileen Pun, Kirsty Irving, Emma Jones, Michael Hulse, Declan Ryan and Claire Trevién. Finally I need to thank the people without whom I would do nothing: Jenny Holden, Chris Larkin and my parents.

Acknowledgements

The mason says: Rocks
happen by chance.
— BASIL BUNTING *'Briggflatts'*

Lubbock's Box

being a cabinet of bird specimens collected
by the naturalist and politician John Lubbock

The way he arranged them
   you'd think he wanted
them to fight instead of fly.
The sharpness of the beaks,
   the brightness of the feathers
battle. Two types of toucans
that never should have met
   stand together. Hummingbirds,
in every size, bluebirds and birds
that are blue: placed, glued.
   Their bills grasp fake fruit
or impale closeted air. There's
not enough space for them all,
   in a cabinet, in Kent.
They must compete to survive,
to be seen. Their wings ache with
   holding still, their colours
cannot take any more eyes:
they burn. (We lost the key).
   Stuffed with arsenic,
with mercury, pests and time
shall not eat them, much—
   We lost the key. And anyway,
if we set them free the poisons escape
along with all the birds
   of North and South America—
well, not all, but more
than I could have imagined or named.

Rhododendron

for my father, who is usually right

It was named for Cecil Rhodes, you said,
may have had other names on other tongues.
But I have since found that it means 'rose-tree'.
They need acidity in the soil, you told me.

The mulch of old leaves and earth we walk on
is enough. The chance or thought that made this be
is irrelevant here, where conditions are right
or else there would not be this full colouring.

Every bloom now is a massive cupped handful.
There is a pink so deep it could be called everlasting.
You wonder, still, how it got here. And how did we?
Arise, tree. The roots are Latin, the origin Nepalese.

St Jerome and the Chaffinch

Usually with a lion he can't shake off,
and always with a book—but,
sometimes, he appears with a chaffinch.

Animals love him. And it's a symbol
of celibacy to be accompanied by a chaffinch.
The colourful male winters less far away than his mate.

He becomes known as the bachelor bird
and also the harbinger of rain.
But only sometimes does he sing for rain,

other times he sings for sun, or for his mate.
The French say *gay comme un pinson*
but we are not always so gay

or so serious. Bosch paints him this way.
I cannot say why he sings, only that
the chaffinch, sometimes, appears with St Jerome.

Maldives

for Phil

It was there you first had Bacardi,
and now it takes you back.
That first sip is the sun on your face.
The last is your foot in the road; unsteady.

The rains brought the toads.
They must have always been there,
but now they made your path
a creaking, slippery bone-mash.

Big Kev hated that, his weight being
an inglorious, crunching death to toads.
One day he painted each amphibian
white, so they showed in the dark.

A kindness. Unable to bear, like the little
glinting bodies, the knowledge drawn from
the sole of the shoe, foot, and its
connected parts' cumulative pressure.

The lacquer, or something in it, killed them.
They littered the street like crumpled tissues.
No crunch. As though their clockwork
had wound down, they stayed stopped.

The Cormorants

You scan the bay and always see one—
plumped like a discarded coat on some
purposeful post of sea-bleached wood.

Oil-black, slick—yet slightly scragged
around the neck, set down without care
and ready, because there is no space

no then-now or here-there
except that which can be flown through
or dived into with a half-jump

to go deeper, to precisely grasp fish,
water snakes, small eels. If you could see that,
if you could see them underwater,

being a different shape,
then this world would not be as it is.
They cry out to the city leaveleave

or nothingisasitseems. Offcuts of night—
for the night is made of them,
is when they come in squalls to the coast

and rest outside your window.
Your hair dried wiry with salt air
you pretend not to notice them,

watch TV. They're there again in the morning
appearing as hastily hung hats.
You see them extend their necks, preen themselves

or stand spread-winged for a second
blazon onto your eye like a motto
—you point one out to me,

say, *Ilovethecormorants, they are alwaysthere.*

Badger

He looked at me and remembered then
that when he was young he wanted nothing
more than to see a human. To see one really.

He paused and stared straight at me,
as if he once wished this happening,
as though in youth all his dreams

were of humans, all his nightmares
of human-baiting. He stopped
and then he ran

on four legs, as something ugly but unusual runs
flatfooted and denser than night—
as if he could run out of my memory

he ran home, in his mind crying
(till he found another thing in motion)
I saw a woman, a woman.

A real woman. He wondered if I too
told the noise of geese and the eerie
sheep's backsides behind the walls

what had stood for a moment opposite in the street.
He wondered if I cried a badger, a badger
stopping and running

because I can not believe
until it is said. Though when said
human/badger doesn't capture

a second's stare at something you once again
can begin to credit breathes and reeks
somewhere in the dark.

Natural History

*'Where the men of science wear their eternity
with the attitude of saints or giants.'*

Here in the least lit corner of the museum
your skin is an affectation. Your hair dulls
and your eye-sockets deepen. You collect
shadow, the clatter of feet, polished rock,

ironwork, stuttered light through tiny panes.
See the joins. Latin erected into names,
stumbles into steps, nature-narrative,
origin-extinction, entrance-exit. Out,

your fat tongue works once more.
We step into sunlight, midday's Oxford
traffic of flesh and thought, and hear:
Every day, till the day I die, I will always . . .

The Safe Harbour

*Flora MacDonald died at Kingsburgh on Skye, in the
same bed in which Bonnie Prince Charlie had slept.*

THE CROSSING

Decanted from the vessel of the corset
the would-be immortal sheds his strange armour
to sleep, and round his body wraps the foreign sheet.

Loosened, his flesh takes the form of the bed.
A new ship, her maiden voyage.
The crossing is a good one, seas smooth as linen,
crews civil as machinery.
At daybreak he hits solid land
with the screaming of the hull against the rocks

and the striking of clocks.
For a moment he is forgotten
and then he finds his feet, where he had
neglected to take them off, in his haste.

FLORA, DUTIFUL

He was to have her bed,
and some petulant part of her
saw him taking it up under his arm
and running away with it
like a wife he would have for himself.

But it was to be his
one night only, a single berth.

FLORA, IN FOREIGN SOIL

When she had taken other beds, forced
to remember sleep in gaol
or keeping it as a custom in the new world,
she had a waking dream first.
A preamble, where that room was but an antechamber
and there was another room, and
her bed behind a night-coloured screen,
sheets as clean as before the birthing.
She blows out the stars clumps at a time
as though a dandelion clock.

FLORA/FAUNA

Mice droppings and bloodstains. There is
much that once lived; animal presence in her bed.

The sharps of goosefeather and fingernail.
Breathing of horses that comes to men with sleep.

Colourless lifemasks of spiders, brief as silk.
Miscellaneous cells strewn like petals on a wedding day.

Pressed beetles light and dulled as paper.
Bugs fattened on the warmth of sleeping weight.

Courtesy of lavender left on the pillow like hair,
to drive out the smells of this world.

FLORA, ON HER DEATHBED

she thinks the bed is narrowing
but then that it is only
the swelling of the wave beneath
that will carry her over
if it does not take her under

the little bed is buoyant
she is singing like a sailor
and her hair has shaken free of its roots
like a flower on water

Great Tit

that see me seeme seeme
makes me want to see

the bird that makes the news
sings louder in cities

flaunts its plumage
has been known to murder bats

flirtatious, unfaithful
divorce is common

and a means to survival
see me seeme seeme

the colourful titmouse
says the medieval bestiary

is a bird curious about other birds

whether dead or alive
they'll come to look

not because they care
because they are curious

they think the world is a mirror or a book

and thus we may catch them
while they search for their selves

Pigeon

At first, I thought it the most delicious noise.
Lodged in our loft it held forth its music,
one strain, over and over—as though there were nothing
in the world but song, babies, cake and nappies.

Friday, I'm half mad and cannot get out of bed.
The bird is nesting somewhere in our insulation,
perhaps she is so fat she cannot get out.
I wonder if she will ever leave.

By next week I will know nothing.
My heart will thrill like a tuning fork,
and I will issue forth one sound forever—
feeling love, love and love and love.

Snow

Overnight it has fallen again.
The blackbirds hop in relief
against the light fracturing surface.
Today is new. When it looks like that

the matter is settled. The many many-

bulbed egg-timers of precipitation
and flowing-back are turned. Snow
edges away from the front door.
The path is where it has always been.

To a Woodpecker

That raucous bunch of ventricles they call
a nest, tapped into the trunk of a birch,
six metres up, its calling to you loud
and constant as pain. I fear if I can,
some bad bird might hear. That sound is scream
then squawk then squabble. It hardens, darkens
to a pupil. Each squeak a mouth, each mouth
made beak, each beak a stomach and a pair
of bald wings—I saw some once, some baby
birds; they looked like my most quoted organ
(and all hearts and baby birds are the same).

Two weeks and your harried motherhood's over.
They're fledged, all gone, or dead. I meant to count
them out, I meant, but the sound grew less, less.

Belle Isle

for the rightful heir

It's the finches that own our line of vision—
flippant between sky and foliage,
holding the gaze with flashes
of umber and lime, glancing
through the imported
blooms.

Sprinkled
from the
tower,
vines
overhang.

Children
call to themselves.

The island is privately
owned—but they're picking it back,
each twig by beak and darts of determined
brightness. Brilliant gold and green, your nail-
varnish catches the sunlight. Laughter erodes lines
like an inland tide, and the finches flit again across the mind.

Species

*'I think he saw that there was a sense of immortality
in having a dinosaur named after your family.'*
— PAUL SERENO

When I picked through Father's things,
some of the structure of his life
seemed missing. Half had been plundered,
but most had been shed along the way.

Not enough evidence to piece together
how this creature once lived.
There were arguments over the way
he carried himself. Stories mutated.

His memory died out before he did.
The fact was he changed. As soon
as we opened it up, the attic and everything in it
started to fade. Nothing survives sunlight,

which only serves to show the dust,
borne by the breathing to cover the past.
Newspaper tans, crumbles at the folds.
Photos blanch to bone. And this

is all that remains. It lives
though it means something new:
RAPTOREX KRIEGSTEINI
Nothing like him really. Smaller. And before.

A Flightless Bird

and this suits you, so you stay
dead as, develop a sternum
insufficient to sustain flight.

Sluggard. You settle down,
having no predators. Perhaps
because you taste so bad.

Loathsome bird. And there's
no such thing as a white dodo.
There's no such thing as dodos.

Fool, crazy, knot-arse. Your call, dodo.
The world just changed around you,
and you nested on the ground.

The Paragliders

arched above the crags and heights
they mimic the easy flight of large birds
twisting in a show of love or hate
or caught in the same updraft—
they turn and sink and lift, as though gravity
is something that will wait, will keep

even as apes we must have wished
to be up there instead, have strained necks
to see and started then to imagine it—
a difference between ourselves and the land
a buffer of air, taut fingers glancing at clouds
the world below understood in green and blue

if you're walking there beneath those
that have by birthday, holiday or anniversary
come to inhabit the sky, beware:
for that which falls in bundles is new
like those borne in the beaks of birds
and that which comes skittering to the ground

at your feet, forgetting how to walk,
is yours and yours to deal with
its cracked eggshell conscience and all—
their memory of flight will not leave them
no matter how you shade their eyes from the sun,
how long you rock them in your featherless arms

Echolocation

if you wait   by the river
they'll come   they know
where you stand   better than you
won't tangle   in your hair
anymore than they would   knot themselves in a tree
you are still   as tree, stone
as predictable   as the current
they only prey   on flying things
they have rules of conduct   fair play, a battle of wings
they pluck an insect   from the surface
you blink at the puckered   point, a place of absence
train your eye to   their trajectory
their sound locks   you to the ground
you cannot even hear it but   it makes you where you are

Familiar Things

The hedge is glossed, and the blackbird in it.
His throat gutters. I hold the rain still to hear.

The tarmac looks like wet paint on a child's picture.
Though the thought dries dull, for an afternoon like this

you'd do it all again. Again try to save the mouse
your cat got. And we'd all learn, again, to build houses.

Notes

BELLE ISLE is the largest island on Windermere and the
only one ever to be inhabited.

SPECIES is based upon the discovery in 2009 of Raptorex
Kriegsteini, a smaller predecessor of the T-Rex, which
was named after the man who illegally smuggled it from
China and handed it over to palaeontologists at the
University of Chicago.

A FLIGHTLESS BIRD is mainly composed of the various
etymological explanations for the name 'dodo'.